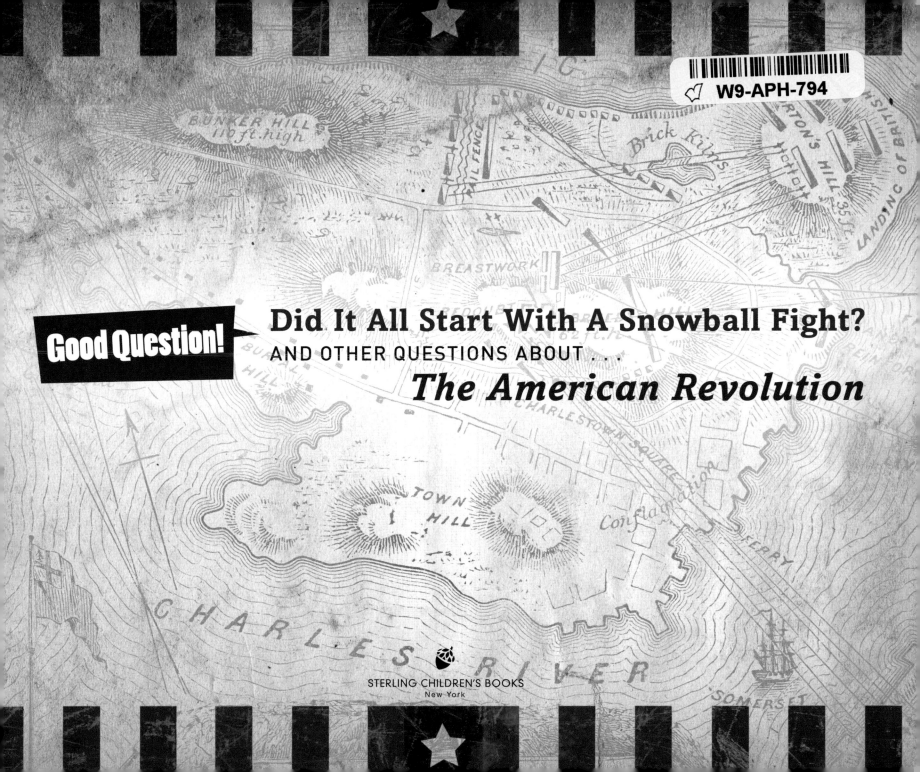

Good Question!

Did It All Start With A Snowball Fight?
AND OTHER QUESTIONS ABOUT . . .
The American Revolution

STERLING CHILDREN'S BOOKS
New York

STERLING CHILDREN'S BOOKS
New York

An Imprint of Sterling Publishing
387 Park Avenue South
New York, NY 10016

Text © 2012 by Mary Kay Carson
Illustrations © 2012 Sterling Publishing Co., Inc.
Photo Credits: Corbis: © Bettmann/CORBIS: 7, © CORBIS: 28 right, © Gianni Dagli Orti/CORBIS: 30, © Heritage Images/Corbis: 31 top; istock: 1, 32; Getty Images: 31 bottom;
Granger Collection NYC: 16, 19, 25, 28 left; Library of Congress, Prints & Photographs Division: [LC-DIG-ppmsc-02751] 13.

ISBN 978-1-4027-8734-8 (paperback)
ISBN 978-1-4027-9626-5 (hardcover)

Library of Congress Cataloging-in-Publication Data

Carson, Mary Kay.
 Did it all start with a snowball fight? : and other questions about the
American Revolution / by Mary Kay Carson.
   p. cm. -- (Who knew?)
 Includes bibliographical references.
 ISBN 978-1-4027-8734-8 (pbk. : alk. paper) -- ISBN 978-1-4027-9626-5 1.
United States--History--Revolution, 1775-1783--Juvenile literature. I. Title.
 E208.C315 2012
 973.3--dc23
                        2011019963

Distributed in Canada by Sterling Publishing
c/o Canadian Manda Group, 165 Dufferin Street
Toronto, Ontario, Canada M6K 3H6
Distributed in the United Kingdom by GMC Distribution Services
Castle Place, 166 High Street, Lewes, East Sussex, England BN7 1XU
Distributed in Australia by Capricorn Link (Australia) Pty. Ltd.
P.O. Box 704, Windsor, NSW 2756, Australia

Design by Elizabeth Phillips
Paintings by Robert Hunt

For information about custom editions, special sales, and premium and corporate purchases, please contact
Sterling Special Sales at 800-805-5489 or specialsales@sterlingpublishing.com.

Manufactured in China
Lot #:
2 4 6 8 10 9 7 5 3 1
05/12

www.sterlingpublishing.com/kids

Did it all start with a snowball fight?

On a winter day in 1770, a crowd gathered on King Street in Boston, Massachusetts. Back then, Massachusetts was not a state. It was a colony controlled by the British Empire. The colonists, the people who lived there, were angry at the British king. They thought they were being mistreated. The king had sent thousands of British soldiers to keep the peace, and the colonists were sick of them. Soldiers outnumbered colonists four to one! The soldiers acted like they owned the place! The Boston colonists were fed up.

The colonists on King Street shouted at a group of soldiers. They yelled nasty names, and some threw snowballs and chunks of ice. Soon the angry crowd grew into a dangerous mob. Hundreds of people circled the British soldiers. The mob pushed in closer and threw oyster shells and rocks. Then someone yelled, "Fire!" The panicked soldiers pointed their guns at the crowd. Shots sounded. When the smoke cleared, five people were dead or dying. Two were teenage boys.

The colonists called the shootings the Boston Massacre. The Boston Massacre and other events sparked a revolt that lead to the American Revolution. That war would end British control of the colonies and create a new nation, the United States of America.

What is a colony and why would you want one?

In 1760, the British Empire was the world's largest empire. It controlled parts of Canada, the Caribbean, India, and thirteen colonies in America. King George III ruled all of it, including 2.5 million colonists. They had to obey Britain's laws and play by its rules.

A colony is like a business owned by a country. Running a faraway colony is not easy—or cheap. So why do it? Colonies helped the British Empire grow richer and more powerful. The New England Colonies had trees for lumber and an ocean nearby for fishing. Connecticut, Massachusetts, New Hampshire, and Rhode Island built ships for the British Empire. The Middle Colonies were Delaware, New Jersey, New York, and Pennsylvania. Farmers grew corn, wheat, and other crops that Britain bought. Southern Colonies also supplied goods to the British Empire. Tobacco came from Maryland and Virginia. North Carolina, South Carolina, and Georgia sold rice and indigo, a plant for dyeing cloth blue.

The colonies sold goods to the British and they bought British goods. In fact, American colonists were only allowed to sell their crops and products to Britain. On top of that, they were only allowed to buy what they could not make from Britain. Some of the things they bought were sugar, cloth, and tea. All the strict rules made some of the colonists really angry. By the 1760s, some of them were mad enough to throw snowballs—and rocks.

This map shows
the thirteen
original colonies.

The tea-dumping colonists didn't want to be recognized, so they dressed themselves as Mohawks—American Indians who lived nearby.

Why get steaming mad over cold tea?

On the night of December 16, 1773, the docks in Boston harbor were dark but not empty. Shadowy figures sneaked along the shore. A group of men and boys were climbing onto anchored British ships full of tea. The raiders broke open 342 chests of tea and dumped each one into the sea. Their protest became known as the Boston Tea Party.

The Boston Tea Party was a message for King George. The colonists didn't like his rules. Americans were only allowed to buy British goods. Want to drink tea? British East India tea was your only choice. And you had to pay whatever taxes, or additional fees, Britain added on. Why should a faraway king be able to tax and control them? Colonists protested the tea tax by refusing to buy or drink tea—and dumping it into harbors.

King George decided to punish the protesting colonists. He outlawed public meetings. Colonies could no longer pick their own sheriffs or judges, and governors answered only to him. The stricter rules made the colonists mad enough to take action. In September 1774, every colony except Georgia sent men to Philadelphia. Fifty-six men went to the secret gathering, including John Adams, Patrick Henry, and George Washington. The meeting was called the First Continental Congress. They promised to cut off trade with Britain. They discussed forming fighting groups, called militias. No one talked about independence from the empire, though. They just wanted Britain to get rid of certain laws—and taxes.

Minutemen took aim hidden behind trees and stone walls.

How long did it take a minuteman to join the fight?

After the First Continental Congress, many colonies organized citizens into militias. Some militiamen were called minutemen. Why? Because they were ready to fight in a minute! They sure showed up right on time on April 18, 1775.

That night 700 British soldiers marched toward Concord, Massachusetts. Their secret mission was to arrest the rebel leaders and destroy their stored weapons. Somehow, the colonists found out about the plan. Who told? Some believe it was the wife of General Thomas Gage, the king's governor of Massachusetts. General Gage was British born, but Mrs. Margaret Gage was born in New Jersey. Did she warn the rebels about the British mission? We don't know, but the warning worked, no matter who gave it. Three riders on horseback—including Paul Revere—galloped toward Concord. Along the way, they woke up people in towns and farms and told them that British troops were coming.

By the time the king's soldiers marched through Lexington on April 19th, seventy or more local minutemen were waiting. Shots were fired, and eight minutemen were killed. The British marched on toward Concord. Many more minutemen waited for them there—in hiding. The local men and boys shot at the king's army, who wore red coats. Sneak attacks were new to them. Hundreds of British troops were killed and wounded as they ran back the way they came. Militiamen had driven the world's most powerful army back to Boston. The fight was on.

Did independence make sense for the colonists?

Not at first. Starting a new country is not easy. Could the thirteen colonies really get by without Britain? The Second Continental Congress met in May 1775. Most men at the meeting still hoped to work out their problems with King George. But British troops had taken over Boston, and George Washington wanted them gone—now. So he put together the Continental army and started raiding British forts to get weapons.

This made King George extra mad. On August 23, 1775, he said all the colonies were in revolt. He said the Continental Congress was an illegal group run by criminals. The British government closed all American ports. Colonists could not buy goods from other countries or sell their crops and lumber to them. King George believed that cutting the colonies off would force them to give up their fight. But it didn't. Instead American colonists began to wonder if maybe they'd be better off without Britain.

Should the colonies make their own country? Colonial rebel and writer Thomas Paine wrote a popular pamphlet called *Common Sense*. It said that, "a government of our own is our natural right." His words changed minds, including those in the Continental Congress. On July 4, 1776, congress accepted the Declaration of Independence. The United States was born. But it was far from free. The new nation would have to fight for independence from Britain. The American Revolution was on.

The Declaration of Independence announced that America would no longer be ruled by Britain.

Who were the Redcoats?

The British soldiers who fought for the king were called Redcoats. They came from England, Scotland, Ireland, and Wales. The colonists teased the king's soldiers in their bright red jackets, calling them "Redcoats" and "lobster backs." Redcoats were well trained as foot soldiers, horse-riding cavalrymen, and grenade-tossing grenadiers.

The British did not fight alone in America. King George paid German soldiers called Hessians to fight, too. Some colonists joined the Redcoats and fought for the king. Not everyone in America wanted to be free of Britain. A number of escaped slaves and American Indians also chose the British side. Troops totaling 50,000 battled against the Continental army. Feeding, arming, moving, and managing so many soldiers so far from home was difficult. Equipment, uniforms, food, and guns arrived on ships from the Empire. But there was not enough to go around, and the British troops often stole food from colonists. And the colonists also had to feed British soldiers and let them stay in their houses.

Who joined the Continental army and why did they look so scruffy?

Hessian leader Johann Rall called the soldiers of the Continental army "country clowns" because they looked so mismatched and messy! Continental army soldiers wore jackets dyed the color of blue jeans. Some didn't even have uniforms. Decent clothes, boots, and food were scarce. Weapons, bullets, and the metal to make them were hard to come by, too. Patriot supporters toppled a lead statue of King George in New York and melted it into 42,088 bullets.

Getting men and boys to join the Continental army was a struggle, too. Promises of free land after the war got many to sign up. Posters showing adventure and excitement brought in teenagers as young as sixteen. Minutemen and other local militias joined with the Continental army when Redcoats threatened their towns. Local militias often included boys and old men, who only fought for a few weeks or months. Washington rarely had enough troops. American troops not only fought a bigger and better trained British army—they also fought hunger, cold, and disease during much of the war.

These boys are making fun of a man loyal to the king by calling him a Tory. The name Tories came from a political group in England.

Why were Tories a royal pain in the Revolution?

Because they supported the king! Colonists who wanted to stay part of Britain were called Royalists, Loyalists, or Tories. About a third of all colonists sided with Britain. Why? Many new arrivals thought of themselves as British subjects of King George. Other Loyalists just didn't want trouble from British soldiers. Besides, living in a United States of America might be worse. Many Loyalists did not think that the colonies could run their own country.

Many people living in the Middle and Southern Colonies were Loyalists, including New Yorkers. New York City was called the Tory capital of America. Loyalists helped the British army by joining up or spying for it. Loyalists showed Redcoats the safest travel routes. Others gave British troops food, horses, and places to stay. To supporters of independence, Loyalists were the dangerous enemy next door. In some regions, Loyalists could not vote or buy or sell land, and had to pay extra U.S. taxes. Some Loyalist homes and farms were robbed and burned. Other Loyalists were put into jail, and even hanged as traitors.

About 500,000 slaves lived in the colonies during the American Revolution. Thousands escaped to British camps when they were promised freedom for fighting for the king. The battlefield seemed better than slavery to them. American Indians took their chances with the British, too. Iroquois, Seneca, and other tribes fought alongside the Redcoats in exchange for keeping colonists out of their lands.

Were Yankee Doodles really dandy?

British troops poked fun at Americans by calling them Yankee Doodles. It meant uneducated, dirty, country hicks—the opposite of smart, fancy-dressed, "dandy" gentlemen. By the end of the Revolution, Americans had turned the insult into a nickname. They proudly called themselves Yankee Doodles, and thought themselves quite dandy, too.

Not everyone wanted to be American. Only a third or so of the colonists supported breaking away from Britain. Those who did called themselves Patriots, or people who support their country. Rebels, outlaws, and traitors were what Loyalists called them. Lots of Patriots lived in the New England Colonies and Pennsylvania. They supported the American Revolution in many ways. Patriots flew the new flag of red and white stripes with thirteen stars. Patriot storeowners did not sell British goods, like cloth or tea. Coffee or "liberty tea," made from mint or other local herbs, was the drink of Patriots. Patriot women wove homemade cloth, fed Continental soldiers, and sewed their uniforms.

Patriots were mainly colonists whose families had come from Europe. Only a few American Indian groups sided with their colonist neighbors. Eventually, the Continental army also offered slaves freedom for fighting. Some slaves chose the Patriot side because Americans valued freedom. Surely slavery wouldn't be legal in a nation founded on liberty, right? This turned out true for New England. But people would be enslaved in the southern states for almost another hundred years.

The song "Yankee Doodle" was popular during the American Revolution.

Washington and Lafayette fought side by side against the British.

What if you didn't take sides?

A third of the colonists were Loyalists, and a third Patriots. That left a third who did not take sides. Religious groups, like the Quakers and Mennonites, believe fighting in wars is wrong. They did not participate. Other colonists were too busy trying to feed their families to care. Farmers and tradesmen worried about life regardless of who won the war. Would someone besides the British buy their rice or wheat? Would people have money to spend in shops? Some switched back and forth between sides during the war. Their loyalties changed with their customers, relatives, bosses—or whomever was winning. Even families did not always agree. Ben Franklin's son, William Franklin, was the Royal governor of New Jersey. William was a Loyalist even though his father was a famous Patriot. William Franklin moved to England with a group of Loyalists toward the end of the war. He never saw his father again.

What do you call the enemy of an enemy?

The enemy of an enemy is a friend. France's leaders wanted victory over the mighty British Empire, its longtime enemy. That meant France was America's friend. It was a secret friendship at first, with France sneaking gifts of gunpowder and money to the Patriots. Then, in 1778, France and America became official friends. France promised to help the Continental army win the American Revolution. French troops, weapons, and warships arrived in America. More than 12,000 French soldiers fought with the Patriots. The French nobleman and military general Marquis de Lafayette fought in the war and helped train new Patriot soldiers. Lafayette and Washington became close friends, winning battles together.

Muskets and rifles had to be reloaded after each shot. A lead ball and gunpowder were dropped into the barrel and then packed down with a long rod.

What weapons did the soldiers use?

The soldiers of the American Revolution fought with muskets, rifles, and cannons. Cannons shot balls filled with burning gunpowder hundreds of feet. Muskets and rifles were guns with long barrels. Both guns could only fire once before the soldier had to reload. Rifles hit faraway targets better, but muskets were much faster to reload. A trained soldier could load and fire a musket three times in one minute. It takes a rifleman at least a minute and a half to load just once.

Battles of that time were fought out in the open. Two enemy armies marched toward each other, like chess pieces on a board. Soldiers stood shoulder to shoulder in rows, one row behind the other. Their muskets were not very accurate, so they waited to see "the whites of their enemy's eyes" before firing. Once the armies got close enough, men fought with long, sharp knives attached to their gun barrels, called bayonets.

How did soldiers fight on the battlefield?

Instead of marching toward the British in rows, some Patriot fighters used the tools of a guerrilla fighter—surprise, speed, and tricks. Patriots sometimes sneaked into British camps at night. Minutemen fired from behind trees and hid under bridges, ambushing Redcoats on the march. Fighting like this was unusual in the 1700s—British troops were not trained for it. Guerrilla-style fighting was something the smaller American army could do better than the world's most powerful military. It gave them an edge.

Did the fighting go on all through the year?

Battles between the Redcoats and Patriots continued off and on for eight years. But during winter, cold weather and snow made moving troops and equipment impossible. Soldiers spent the winter months in camps—working to survive and waiting for spring to restart the war. They built cabins, cut firewood, and trained. Often troops didn't have enough clothing and some walked barefoot through the snow. Sometimes there was so little food that soldiers ate roasted pieces of leather and chewed on sticks. Smallpox and other sickness killed many cold and hungry soldiers.

Where was the action?

Fighting went on throughout the thirteen colonies and Canada, another British colony. Land battles between musket-armed soldiers often happened the same time battleships fought along the coast. But the fighting did move during the war's eight years. It went from north to south. Many of the first battles of the American Revolution were fought in Massachusetts and other parts of New England. By 1777, the fighting had moved to the Middle Colonies, where the Redcoats controlled both Philadelphia and New York City. Losses in New York, New Jersey, and Pennsylvania nearly defeated Washington's Continental army.

Then, in 1778, France entered the war and sent its powerful navy toward the northern colonies. Britain did not want to fight the French navy, so the Redcoats left Philadelphia, stopped attacking in the North, and moved to the South. In December 1778, British troops sailed to the Georgia coast and captured the city of Savannah. Southern Colonies, such as the Carolinas and Virginia, saw most of the fighting toward the end of the war.

The long winter of 1777–1778 was extra harsh in Valley Forge, Pennsylvania. By the time spring arrived, nearly 2,500 of General Washington's 10,000 men were dead from hunger, cold, and disease.

How many battles did it take to win the war?

Too many. Thousands and thousands of soldiers died in the American Revolution—both British and American. A thousand Redcoats died or were wounded at Bunker Hill, Massachusetts, in 1775. The 1777 Pennsylvania battles of Brandywine and Germantown caused more than a thousand casualties on both sides. And a thousand Americans died or were injured at the 1780 Battle of Camden in South Carolina. Disease, cold, hunger, and prison camps killed tens of thousands more. When would it end?

By 1781, Virginia was a battleground. That fall, a French fleet sailed toward its coast. Washington knew they would keep British troops from escaping by sea. He saw a chance to trap the Redcoats. Washington led his army toward the coastal port of Yorktown, where 7,500 British troops were stationed. French foot soldiers rushed southward to join them. Soon trenches, or large ditches, full of soldiers surrounded the British army. About 18,000 French and American soldiers and sailors fenced in the Redcoats. British general Lord Charles Cornwallis and his men were trapped.

On October 17, 1781, a British drummer boy appeared atop a trench wall. He beat a drum to get everyone's attention. Then an officer climbed out of the same trench waving a white handkerchief. The British were surrendering. Soldiers put down their muskets and the British band played "The World Turned Upside Down." The Patriots' victory at Yorktown was the beginning of the long war's end.

This unfinished painting shows those Americans who negotiated the Treaty of Paris. The British group refused to pose.

The Treaty of Paris

Article 10.

Done at Paris

D. Hartley

John Adams

B Franklin

John Jay

How did the underdog Patriots come out on top?

When the ink had dried on the Declaration of Independence, the British Empire had the planet's most powerful military. All the colonists had were minutemen and other militias. How were the Patriots able to win? The British had more troops and more supplies. But it took a long time for soldiers and supplies to make the journey across the Atlantic Ocean. The Patriots could sign up soldiers from next door. And these local fighters had an advantage. Knowing every hill, valley, bridge, and shortcut path helped them plot sneak attacks. The British did not know their way around and were not trained in guerilla warfare. Plus once France started fighting in the colonies, the British military was spread very thin. Not having enough troops made British soldiers feel hopeless about the war. Many did not think it was worth the fight, so they did not try very hard. In contrast, Washington and other Patriot leaders were eager to fight for their liberty and freedom. For them there was no doubt that the war was worth it!

Fighting went on for two years after Britain's surrender at Yorktown. Finally, British lawmakers decided to talk peace. The war in America was too expensive and used up troops needed elsewhere in their empire. France hosted the talks and the final agreement was called the Treaty of Paris. The Treaty of Paris said that America was no longer a colony and that Britain accepted its independence. The agreement also drew the new nation's borders. The United States went west to the Mississippi River, north to Canada, east to the Atlantic Ocean, and south to Florida. The warring countries, one ancient and one newborn, signed it on September 3, 1783. Two months later, the last Redcoats left New York City.

The French Revolution that threw King Louis out of his castle was inspired by the American colonists seeking freedom. The ideas of liberty and equality helped bring rights and freedoms to all people.

Were the shots fired at Lexington and Concord "heard round the world"?

The poet Ralph Waldo Emerson said they were. In truth, not even Boston heard that gunfire. But the ideas behind the American Revolution did travel. As a country that had fought for its independence, America changed the rules. Ordinary citizens got involved in politics—they voiced their opinions, gave ideas, and helped make decisions.

As the decades passed, the example of the American Revolution moved people to continue to push for change in the United States. Beliefs in liberty and equality brought the end of slavery, gave women the right to vote, and protected civil rights.

The American Revolution inspired other colonies and countries around the world to fight for their independence too. The French Revolution overthrew King Louis in 1792, less than a decade after the Treaty of Paris. Freedom, liberty, and equality were once just ideas held by protesting Patriots. Now they are human values all over the world.

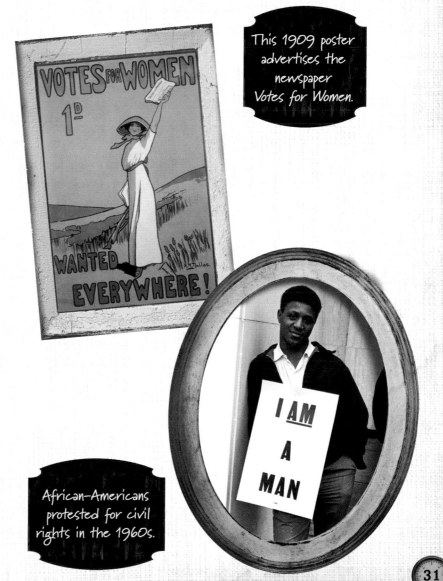

This 1909 poster advertises the newspaper Votes for Women.

African-Americans protested for civil rights in the 1960s.

AMERICAN REVOLUTION TIMELINE

1770   MARCH 5   Five American colonists die in the Boston Massacre in Massachusetts.

1773   DECEMBER 16   Colonists raid British ships during the Boston Tea Party.

1774   SEPTEMBER   First Continental Congress meets in Philadelphia, Pennsylvania.

1775   APRIL 19   Minutemen and British soldiers fight the Battles of Lexington and Concord in Massachusetts.
        MAY   Second Continental Congress meets; George Washington becomes leader of the Continental army.
        AUGUST 23   King George III declares the American colonies to be in illegal revolt.

1776   JULY 4   The Continental Congress accepts the Declaration of Independence, creating the United States.
        DECEMBER 26   General Washington crosses the Delaware river with troops and wins the Battle of Trenton in New Jersey.

1777   **Fighting moves from New England to the Middle Colonies.**
        SEPTEMBER 11   The British win the Battle of Brandywine in Pennsylvania.
        OCTOBER 4   Washington's troops are defeated in the Battle of Germantown in Pennsylvania.
        DECEMBER 19   Washington's army arrives at Valley Forge, Pennsylvania and spends the winter.

1778   FEBRUARY 6   The United States and France become allies.
        DECEMBER 29   The British capture Savannah, Georgia.

1779   **Fighting moves to the Southern Colonies.**

1780   AUGUST 16   The British win the Battle of Camden in South Carolina, killing or injuring a thousand Patriot soldiers.

1781   SEPTEMBER 5   French battleships attack British ships along Virginia's coast.
        OCTOBER 19   British General Cornwallis surrenders at Yorktown, Pennsylvania.

1782   **Britain and America discuss peace; some fighting continues.**

1783   SEPTEMBER 3   The United States and Great Britain sign a peace treaty in Paris, ending the American Revolution.

For bibliography and further reading visit: http://www.sterlingpublishing.com/kids/good-question